The Magic of Joy

A GARLAND OF HAPPY THOUGHTS
WITH WHICH TO GREET
EACH MERRY DAY!

Compiled by Louise Bachelder

GIFTS OF GOLD
———
THE PETER PAUPER PRESS, INC.
MOUNT VERNON, NEW YORK

COPYRIGHT
©
1971
BY THE
PETER
PAUPER
PRESS, INC.

BJ
1481
B3
M3

Joy is not in things; it is in us.

Richard Wagner

The Magic of Joy

TODAY, whatever may annoy,
The word for me is Joy, just simple joy;
The joy of life;
The joy of children and of wife;
The joy of bright, blue skies;
The joy of rain; the glad surprise
Of twinkling stars that shine at night;
The joy of winged things upon their flight;
The joy of noonday, and the tried
True joyousness of eventide;
The joy of labor, and of mirth;

The joy of air, and sea, and earth —
The countless joys that ever flow from Him
Whose vast beneficence doth dim
The lustrous light of day,
And lavish gifts divine upon our way.
   Whate'er there be of Sorrow
   I'll put off till Tomorrow,
And when Tomorrow comes, why then
'Twill be Today and Joy again.
John Kendrick Bangs

THERE are some who possess the magic touch, the infectious spirit of enthusiasm; who have the same effect as a beautiful morning which never reaches noon. Under this spell one's mind is braced, one's spirit recreated; one is ready for any adventure, even if it only be the doing of the next disagreeable task lightheartedly.
Kate Douglas Wiggin

You must wake and call me early, call me early,
   mother dear;
Tomorrow 'ill be the happiest time of all the
   blythe Newyear;
Of all the glad Newyear, mother, the maddest,
   merriest day —
For I'm to be Queen o' the May, mother, I'm
   to be Queen o' the May.

Alfred, Lord Tennyson

To keep one sacred flame
   Through life unchilled, unmoved,
To love in wintry age, the same
   As first in youth we loved,
To feel that we adore
   Even to fond excess
That though the heart would break with more,
   It could not live with less.

Thomas Moore

No enjoyment, however inconsiderable, is confined to the present moment. A man is the happier for life from having made once an agreeable tour, or lived for any length of time with pleasant people, or enjoyed any considerable interval of innocent pleasure.

Sydney Smith

HAPPY the Man, and happy he alone,
   He, who can call today his own:
   He, who, secure within, can say,
Tomorrow do thy worst, for I have liv'd today.
     Be fair, or foul, or rain, or shine,
   The joys I have possess'd, in spite of fate,
     are mine.
Not heav'n itself upon the past has pow'r;
But what has been, has been, and I have had
   my hour.

John Dryden

THE joy of life is to put out one's power in some natural and useful or harmless way. There is no other. And the real misery is not to do this.

Oliver Wendell Holmes, Jr.

WEEPING may endure for a night, but joy cometh in the morning.

Psalms xxx:5

So here I was once more in the role of mountain climber, hunter, artist and writer, my album in my pocket, my gun on my shoulder, my stick in my hand. Surely, to travel is to live in all the meaning of the word; is to forget the past and future in the present; is to breathe the free air, feel the joy of living, to become an integral part of creation.

Alexandre Dumas

WHEN I hear music I fear no danger, I am invulnerable, I see no foe. I am related to the earliest times and to the latest.

Henry David Thoreau

I HEAR you, little bird,
Shouting a-swing above the broken wall.
Shout louder yet; no song can tell it all.
Sing to my soul in the deep, still wood:
'Tis wonderful beyond the wildest word:
I'd tell it, too, if I could.

Oft when the white, still dawn
Lifted the skies and pushed the hills apart,
I've felt it like a glory in my heart —
(The world's mysterious stir)
But had not throat like yours, my bird,
Nor such a listener.

Edwin Markham

I DEVISE to boys, jointly, all the idle fields and commons, where ball may be played, all pleasant waters where one may swim, all snow-clad hills where one may coast, and all streams and ponds where one may fish, or where when Winter comes, one may skate, to have and to hold the same for the period of their boyhood. And all the meadows, with the clover-blossoms and butterflies thereof, the woods with their appurtenances, the birds and squirrels and echoes and strange noises, and all distant places which may be visited, together with the adventures there to be found.

Charles Lounsbury

RICH the treasure,
Sweet the pleasure,
Sweet is pleasure after pain.

John Dryden

IF there are no books in this world, then nothing need be said, but since there are books, they must be read; if there is no wine, then nothing need be said, but since there is wine, it must be drunk; if there are no famous hills, then nothing need be said, but since there are, they must be visited; if there are no flowers and no moon, then nothing need be said, but since there are, they must be enjoyed; if there are no talented men and beautiful women, then nothing need be said, but since there are, they must be loved and protected.

Chang Ch'ao

YOU'VE seen the world —
The beauty and the wonder and the power,
The shapes of things, their colors, lights and
    shades,
Changes, surprises — and God made it all.

Robert Browning

Leave something to wish for, so as not to be miserable from very happiness.

Baltasar Gracián

God sent His singers upon earth
With songs of gladness and of mirth
That they might touch the hearts of men,
And bring them back to heaven again.

Henry Wadsworth Longfellow

Laugh, little fellow, laugh and sing
And just be glad for everything!
Be glad for morning and for night,
For sun and stars that laugh with light,
For trees that chuckle in the breeze,
For singing birds and humming bees —
Be one with them, and laugh along
And weave their gladness in your song.

. . . . . .

Laugh, little fellow, laugh and sing
And coax the joy from everything;
Take gladness at its fullest worth
And make each hour an hour of mirth,
So that when on the downward slope
Of life the radiant sky of hope
Will bend above you all the way
And make you happy, as today.

Wilbur D. Nesbit

Of all the joys that lighten suffering earth, what joy is welcomed like a new-born child?

Caroline Norton

Let us go in once more
By some blue mountain door
And hold communion with the forest leaves.

Bliss Carman

You wake up in the morning, and lo! your purse is magically filled with twenty-four hours of the magic tissue of the universe of your life. No one can take it from you. No one receives either more or less than you receive. Waste your infinitely precious commodity as much as you will, and the supply will never be withheld from you. Moreover, you cannot draw on the future. Impossible to get into debt. You can only waste the passing moment. You cannot waste tomorrow; it is kept for you.

Arnold Bennett

HAPPINESS to me is wine,
Effervescent, superfine.
Full of tang and fiery pleasure,
Far too hot to leave me leisure
For a single thought beyond it.

Amy Lowell

I WANDERED lonely as a cloud
    That floats on high o'er vales and hills,
When all at once I saw a crowd,
    A host of golden daffodils,
Beside the lake, beneath the trees,
Fluttering and dancing in the breeze.
    . . . . .
The waves beside them danced, but they
    Outdid the sparkling waves in glee;
A poet could not but be gay
    In such a jocund company;
I gazed, and gazed, but little thought
What wealth the show to me had brought.

For oft, when on my couch I lie
    In vacant or in pensive mood,
They flash upon that inward eye
    Which is the bliss of solitude;
And then my heart with pleasure fills
And dances with the daffodils.

                        William Wordsworth

Great is he who enjoys his earthenware as if it were plate, and not less great is the man to whom all his plate is no more than earthenware.

Robert Leighton

The exquisite quiet of this room! I have been sitting in utter idleness, watching the sky, viewing the shape of golden sunlight upon the carpet, which changes as the minutes pass, letting my eye wander from one framed print to another, and along the ranks of my beloved books. Within the house nothing stirs. In the garden I can hear singing of birds, I can hear the rustle of their wings....

My house is perfect. Just large enough to allow the grace of order in domestic circumstances; just that superfluity of intra-mural space, to lack which is to be less at one's ease....

To me, this little room is beautiful, and chiefly because it is home. Through the greater part of life I was homeless....

The unspeakable blessedness of having a home! Much as my imagination has dwelt upon it for thirty years, I never knew how deep and exquisite a joy could lie in the assurance that one is at home for ever.

George Gissing

NONE of us yet know what fairy palaces we may build of beautiful thoughts — proof against all adversity. Bright fancies, satisfied memories, noble histories, faithful sayings, precious and restful thoughts, which care cannot disturb, nor pain make gloomy — houses built without hands, for our souls to live in.

John Ruskin

Some think the world is made for fun and frolic,
And so do I! And so do I!
Some think it well to be all melancholic,
To pine and sigh, to pine and sigh.
But I, I love to spend my time in singing
Some joyous song, some joyous song;
To set the air with music bravely ringing
Is far from wrong! Is far from wrong!

Hearken! Hearken! Music sounds afar!
Hearken! Hearken! Music sounds afar!
Funiculi, funicula, funiculi, funicula!
Joy is everywhere, funiculi, funicula!

Ah me! 'Tis strange that some should take to sighing,
And like it well! And like it well!
For me, I have not thought it worth the trying,
So cannot tell! So cannot tell!
With laugh, and dance, and song, the day soon passes,

Full soon is gone, full soon is gone;
For mirth was made for joyous lads and lasses
To call their own! To call their own!

Luigi Denza

AND truly, though we were at sea, there was so much to behold and wonder at, to me, who was on my first voyage....

At last we hoisted the stun'-sails up to the topsail yards, and as soon as the vessel felt them, she gave a sort of bound like a horse, and the breeze blowing more and more, she went plunging along, shaking off the foam from her bows like foam from a bridle-bit. Every mast and timber seemed to have a pulse in it that was beating with life and joy, and I felt a wild exulting in my own heart, and felt as if I would be glad to bound along so round the world....

Yes! yes! give me this glorious ocean life, this salt-sea life, this briny, foamy life, when the sea neighs and snorts, and you breathe the very breath that the great whales respire! Let me roll around the globe, let me rock upon the sea, let me race and pant out my life with an eternal breeze astern and an endless sea before!

Herman Melville

When the purple flame shoots up —
    And Love ascends his throne —
I cannot hear your songs — O birds —
    For the witchery of my own.

And every human heart
    Still keeps that golden day,
And rings the bells of jubilee
    On its own First of May.

Ralph Waldo Emerson

The holiest of all holidays are those
Kept by ourselves in silence and apart;
The secret anniversaries of the heart,
When the full river of feeling overflows;
The happy days unclouded to their close;
The sudden joys that out of darkness start
As flames from ashes; swift desires that dart
Like swallows singing down each wind that
   blows.
White as the gleam of a receding sail,
White as the cloud that floats and fades in air,
White as the whitest lily on a stream,
These tender memories are; a fairy tale
Of some enchanted land, we know not where,
But lovely as a landscape in a dream.
Henry Wadsworth Longfellow

The joyfulness of a man prolongeth his days.
Ecclesiasticus XXX:22

For, lo! the winter is past, the rain is over and gone; the flowers appear on the earth; the time of the singing of birds is come, and the voice of the turtle is heard in our land.

Song of Solomon II:11,12

Once more the liberal year laughs out
   O'er richer stores than gems of gold;
Once more with harvest song and shout
   Is nature's boldest triumph told.

John Greenleaf Whittier

Afoot and light-hearted I take to the open road,
Healthy, free, the world before me,
The long brown path before me leading
   wherever I choose.

Walt Whitman

THE crowning fortune of a man is to be born to some pursuit which finds him employment and happiness, whether it be to make baskets, or broadswords, or canals, or statues, or songs.

Ralph Waldo Emerson

LIFE's a pudding full of plums;
Care's a canker that benumbs,
Wherefore waste our elocution
On impossible solution?
Life's a pleasant institution,
Let us take it as it comes!

William S. Gilbert

NOR rural sights, alone, but rural sounds
Exhilarate the spirit and restore
The tone of languid nature.

William Cowper

I USED to like to hear my father, Charles Darwin, admire the beauty of a flower. It was a kind of gratitude to the flower itself, and a personal love for its delicate form and color. I remember him gently touching a flower he delighted in. It was the same simple admiration that a child might have.

Francis Darwin

SOMEWHERE there waiteth in this world of ours
For one lone soul, another lonely soul —
Each chasing each through all the weary hours,
And meeting strangely at one sudden goal;
Then blend they — like green leaves with
   golden flowers,
Into one beautiful and perfect whole —
And life's long night is ended, and the way
Lies open onward to eternal day.

Sir Edwin Arnold

NEVER miss a joy in this world of trouble — that's my theory! . . . Happiness, like mercy, is twice blest: it blesses those most intimately associated with it and it blesses all those who see it, hear it, feel it, touch it or breathe the same atmosphere.

Kate Douglas Wiggin

Go not abroad for happiness. For see!
It is a flower that blossoms by thy door.
Bring love and justice home; and then no more
Thou'lt wonder in what dwelling joy may be.

Minot J. Savage

WHO knows the joys of friendship?
The trust, security, and mutual tenderness,
The double joys where each is glad for both?

Nicholas Rowe

I HAVE fallen into the hands of thieves, what then? They have left me the sun and moon, fire and water, a loving wife and many friends to pity me, and some to relieve me, and I can still discourse; and unless I list, they have not taken away my merry spirit and a good conscience. . . . And he that hath so many causes of joy, and so great, is very much in love with sorrow and peevishness who loses all those pleasures and chooses to sit down on his little handful of thorns.

Jeremy Taylor

How fading are the joys we dote upon!
Like apparitions seen and gone.
But those which soonest take their flight
Are the most exquisite and strong, —
Like angels' visits, short and bright;
Mortality's too weak to bear them long.

John Norris

THE joy of work depends upon the way we meet it — whether we arm ourselves each morning to attack it as an enemy that must be vanquished before night comes, or whether we open our eyes with the sunrise to welcome it as an approaching friend who will keep us delightful company all day, and who will make us feel, at evening, that the day was well worth its fatigues.

Lucy Larcom

You never enjoy the world aright, till the Sea itself floweth in your veins, till you are clothed with the heavens, and crowned with the stars; and perceive yourself to be the sole heir of the whole world, and more than so, because men are in it who are every one sole heirs as well as you. Till you can sing and rejoice and delight in God, as misers do in gold, and Kings in sceptres, you never enjoy the world.

Till your spirit filleth the whole world, and the stars are your jewels; till you are as familiar with the ways of God in all Ages as with your walk and table: till you are intimately acquainted with that shady nothing out of which the world was made: till you love men so as to desire their happiness, with a thirst equal to the zeal of your own; till you delight in God for being good to all: you never enjoy the world. . . .

Thomas Traherne

THE things of every day are all so sweet —
The morning meadows wet with dew,
The dance of daisies in the noon; the blue
Of far-off hills where twilight shadows lie;
The night, with all its tender mysteries of sound
And silence, and God's starry sky!
Oh, life — the whole of life — is far too fleet.
The things of every day are all so sweet.

The common things of life are all so dear —
The waking in the warm half gloom
To find again the old familiar room,
The scents and sights and sounds that never tire;
The homely work, the plans, the lilt of baby's laugh,
The crackle of the open fire;
The waiting, then the footsteps coming near,
The opening door, your hand-clasp — and your kiss —
Is Heaven not after all the Now and Here?
The common things of life are all so dear.

Alice E. Allen

THE air is like a butterfly
   With frail blue wings,
The happy earth looks at the sky
   And sings.

Joyce Kilmer

You say that "this world to you seems drain'd of its sweets!" I don't know what you call sweet. Honey and the honeycomb, roses and violets, are yet in the earth. The sun and moon yet reign in Heaven, and the lesser lights keep up their pretty twinklings. Meats and drinks, sweet sights and sweet smells, a country walk, spring and autumn, follies and repentance, quarrels and reconcilements have all a sweetness by turns. Good humor and good nature, friends at home that love you, and friends abroad that miss you — you possess all these things, and more innumerable, and these are all sweet things. You may extract honey from everything.

Charles Lamb

LAUGHTER is the joyous, universal evergreen of life.

Abraham Lincoln

There be many that have forty times our estates, that would give the greatest part of it to be healthful and cheerful like us; who with the expense of a little money have eat, and drunk, and laughed, and angled, and sung, and slept securely; and rose the next day, and cast away care, and sung, and laughed, and angled again; which are blessings rich men cannot purchase with all their money.

Izaak Walton

My eyes make pictures when they are shut.
Samuel Taylor Coleridge

Nothing cheers me up like having understood something difficult to understand. I should try it more often.

Georg Christoph Lichtenberg

No one can tell but he that loves his children, how many delicious accents make a man's heart dance in the pretty conversation of those dear pledges; their childishness, their stammering, their little angers, their innocence, their imperfections, their necessities are so many little emanations of joy and comfort to him that delights in their persons and society.

Jeremy Taylor

PLEASURES lie thickest where no pleasures seem;
There's not a leaf that falls upon the ground
But holds some joy, of silence or of sound,
Some sprite begotten of a summer dream.
The very meanest things are made supreme
With innate ecstasy. No grain of sand
But moves a bright and million-peopled land,
And hath its Edens and its Eves, I deem.

Samuel Laman Blanchard

Life has loveliness to sell,
    All beautiful and splendid things,
Blue waves whitened on a cliff,
    Soaring fire that sways and sings
And children's faces looking up
Holding wonder like a cup.

Life has loveliness to sell,
    Music like a curve of gold,
Scent of pine trees in the rain,
    Eyes that love you, arms that hold,
And for your spirit's still delight,
Holy thoughts that star the night.

Spend all you have for loveliness,
    Buy it and never count the cost;
For one white singing hour of peace
    Count many a year of strife well lost,
And for a breath of ecstasy
Give all you have been, or could be.

Sara Teasdale

Join the whole creation of animate things in a deep heartfelt joy that you are alive, that you see the sun, that you are in this glorious earth which nature has made so beautiful, and which is yours to conquer and enjoy.

Sir William Osler

My true-love hath my heart and I have his,
By just exchange one for another given:
I hold his dear, and mine he cannot miss,
There never was a better bargain driven:
    My true-love hath my heart, and I have his.

His heart in me keeps him and me in one,
My heart in him his thoughts and senses guides:
He loves my heart, for once it was his own,
I cherish his because in me it bides:
    My true-love hath my heart, and I have his.

Sir Philip Sidney

DESIRE joy and thank God for it. Renounce it, if need be, for others' sake. That's joy beyond joy.... God gives each man one life, like a lamp, then gives that lamp due measure of oil; lamp lighted, hold high, wave wide, its comfort to share.

Robert Browning

How beautiful is the rain!
After the dust and heat,
In the broad and fiery street,
In the narrow lane,
How beautiful is the rain!

Henry Wadsworth Longfellow

MY heart leaps up when I behold
A rainbow in the sky.

William Wordsworth

I lean over the rail of my porch to hear what is in the air, liquid with the blue-bird's warble.

    My life partakes of infinity.

    I go forth to make new demands on life.

    I wish to have my immortality now.

    I am eager to report the glory of the universe.

Henry David Thoreau

Take time to work —
    It is the price of success.
Take time to think —
    It is the source of power.
Take time to play —
    It is the secret of perpetual youth.
Take time to read —
    It is the fountain of wisdom.
Take time to be friendly —
    It is the road to happiness.
Take time to dream —

It is hitching your wagon to a star.
Take time to love and to be loved —
  It is the privilege of the gods.
Take time to look around —
  It is too short a day to be selfish.
Take time to laugh —
  It is the music of the soul.

Old English Prayer

'Twas a jolly old pedagogue, long ago,
  Tall and slender, and sallow and dry;
His form was bent, and his gait was slow,
His long thin hair was white as snow,
  But a wonderful twinkle shone in his eye.
And he sang every night as he went to bed,
  "Let us be happy down here below;
The living should live, though the dead be dead,"
  Said the jolly old pedagogue long ago.

George Arnold

ALL about my garden today the birds are loud. To say that the air is filled with their song gives no idea of the ceaseless piping, whistling, trilling, which at moments ring to heaven in a triumphant unison, a wild accord. Now and then I notice one of the smaller songsters who seems to strain his throat in a madly joyous endeavour to out-carol all the rest. It is a chorus of praise such as none other of earth's children have the voice or heart to utter. As I listen I am carried away by glorious rapture; my being melts in the tenderness of an impassioned joy....

George Gissing

LOVE, then, hath every bliss in store;
'Tis friendship, and 'tis something more.
Each other every wish they give;
Not to know love is not to live.

John Gay

I FIND the gayest castles in the air that were ever piled, far better for comfort and use, than the dungeons in the air that are daily dug and caverned out by the discontented.

Ralph Waldo Emerson

WHEN music spills from golden throat
    In wild bird reveille,
I push the drab world out in space
    And live in melody.
When color glows in countless ways
    Before my hungry eyes,
I am a gourmand at the feast
    Unmindful of how time flies,
For when this pageantry is spread
I quite forget my daily bread.

When cool waves run to greet the sands
    And whisper deep-sea lore,

I stand, at crimson close of day,
    Enchanted on the shore.
Each season wafts in new delights
    As beauty flames its way,
On rock, and earth, and sky, and sea,
    With respite for the day —
And, oh, my dear, I humbly own
I cannot live by bread alone!

Christina G. Rossetti

'Tis not the food, but the content
That makes the table's merriment.
Where trouble serves the board, we eat
The platters there, as soon as meat.
A little pipkin with a bit
Of mutton, or of veal in it,
Set on my table, trouble-free,
More than a feast contenteth me.

Robert Herrick

A CARELESS song, with a little nonsense in it now and then, does not misbecome a monarch.

Horace Walpole

WHEN all the world is young, lad,
    And all the trees are green;
And every goose a swan, lad,
    And every lass a queen;
Then hey, for boot and horse, lad,
    And 'round the world away;
Young blood must have its course, lad,
    And every dog his day.

Charles Kingsley

YOUTH is happy because it has the ability to see beauty. Anyone who keeps the ability to see beauty never grows old.

Franz Kafka

"O *can't* believe impossible things." "I daresay you haven't had much practice," said the Queen. "When I was your age, I always did it for half-an-hour a day. Why, sometimes I've believed as many as six impossible things before breakfast."

Lewis Carroll

My mind to me a kingdom is;
    Such present joys therein I find,
That it excels all other bliss
    That earth affords or grows by kind:
Though much I want which most would have,
Yet still my mind forbids to crave.

Edward Dyer

To have joy one must share it. —
Happiness was born a twin.

Lord Byron

HE has spent his life best who has enjoyed it most. God will take care that we do not enjoy it any more than is good for us.... All of the animals, excepting man, know that the principal business of life is to enjoy it.

Samuel Butler

FOR an empty crown is a bauble,
    And he is a sovereign alone
Who lives to bring joy unto others,
    And to make their trouble his own.

Lucy Larcom

AWAY with funeral music — set
    The pipe to powerful lips —
The cup of life's for him that drinks
    And not for him that sips.

Robert Louis Stevenson

LIFT up one hand to heaven and thank your stars if they have given you the proper sense to enable you to appreciate the inconceivably droll situations in which we catch our fellow creatures.

Sir William Osler

I THOUGHT the sparrow's note from heaven,
Singing at dawn on the alder bough;
I brought him home, in his nest, at even;
He sings the song, but it cheers not now,
For I did not bring home the river and sky; —
He sang to my ear, — they sang to my eye.

Ralph Waldo Emerson

THE mintage of Wisdom is to know that rest is rust, and that Real Life is in Love, Laughter, and Work.

Elbert Hubbard

IF one should give me a dish of sand, and tell me there were particles of iron in it, I might look for them with my eyes, and search for them with my clumsy fingers, and be unable to detect them; but let me take a magnet and sweep through it, and how would it draw to itself the almost invisible particles by the mere power of attraction. — The unthankful heart, like my finger in the sand, discovers no mercies; but let the thankful heart sweep through the day, and as the magnet finds the iron, so it will find, in every hour, some heavenly blessings, only the iron in God's sand is gold!

Henry Ward Beecher

THE laugh of a child will make the holiest day more sacred still. Strike with hand of fire, O weird musician, thy harp strung with Appollo's golden hair; fill the vast cathedral aisles with

symphonies sweet and dim, deft toucher of the organ keys; blow, bugler, blow, until thy silver notes do touch and kiss the moonlit waves, and charm lovers wandering 'mid the vine-clad hills. But know, your sweetest strains are discords all, compared with childhood's happy laugh — the laugh that fills the eyes with light and every heart with joy. O rippling river of laughter, thou art the blessed boundary line between the beasts and men; and every forward wave of thine doth drown some fretful fiend of care. O Laughter, rose-lipped daughter of joy, there are dimples enough in thy cheeks to catch and hold and glorify all the tears of grief.

Robert G. Ingersoll

STAY, stay at home, my heart and rest;
Home-keeping hearts are happiest.

Henry Wadsworth Longfellow

ALL God's pleasures are simple ones: the rapture of a May morning sunshine, the stream blue and green, kind words, benevolent acts, the glow of good humor.

F. W. Robertson

WHEN Time, who steals our years away,
Shall steal our pleasures, too,
The mem'ry of the past will stay,
And half our joys renew.

Thomas Moore

THOUGH the times be dark and dreary,
Though the way be long,
Keep your spirits bright and cheery —
  "Bide a wee, and dinna weary!"
  Is a heartsome song.

John Oxenham

THE whole secret of remaining young in spite of years, . . is to cherish enthusiasm in oneself, by poetry, by contemplation, by charity, that is by the maintenance of harmony in the soul.

Henri-Frédéric Amiel

HOPE not sunshine every hour;
Fear not clouds will always lower.
Happiness is but a name.
Make content and ease thy aim.

Robert Burns

WHO is the happiest of men? He who values the
 merits of others,
And in their pleasure takes joy, even as though
 'twere his own.

Johann Wolfgang von Goethe

LIFE is sweet, brother... There's night and day, brother, both sweet things; sun, moon, and stars, brother, all sweet things; there's likewise the wind on the heath.

George Borrow

I KNOW not what the day may bring,
For now 'tis sorrow that I sing,
   And now, 'tis joy;
In both a Father's hand I see,
For one renews the man in me,
   And one the boy!

John Bannister Tabb

ON with the dance! let joy be unconfined;
No sleep till morn, when Youth and Pleasure meet
To chase the glowing hours with flying feet.

Lord Byron

THERE is, perhaps, no solitary sensation so exquisite as that of slumbering on the grass or hay, shaded from the hot sun by a tree, with the consciousness of a fresh light air running through the wide atmosphere, and the sky stretching far overhead upon all sides.

Leigh Hunt

SEE how that pair of billing doves
With open murmurs own their loves
And, heedless of censorious eyes,
Pursue their unpolluted joys.

Lady Mary W. Montagu

THERE is no beautifier of complexion, or form, or behavior, like the wish to scatter joy and not pain around us.

Ralph Waldo Emerson

I LIKE to rest, whether sitting or lying down, with my heels as high as my head, or higher.

Michel de Montaigne

TAKE joy home,
And make a place in thy great heart for her,
And give her time to grow, and cherish her!
Then will she come and often sing to thee
When thou art working in the furrows; ay,
Or weeding in the sacred hour of dawn.
It is a comely fashion to be glad.
Joy is the grace we say to God.

Jean Ingelow

HE is truly happy who has all that he wishes to have, and wishes to have nothing which he ought not to wish.

St. Augustine

I HOPE succeeding generations will be able to have more leisure time; that they may enjoy their days, and the earth, and the beauty of this beautiful world; that they may rest by the sea and dream; that they may dance and sing, and eat and drink.

Richard Jefferies

LIFE is a romantic business. It is painting a picture, not doing a sum — but you have to make the romance. And it will come to the question how much fire you have in your belly.

Oliver Wendell Holmes, Jr.

FULL of love for all things in the world, practicing virtue, in order to benefit others, this man alone is happy.

Dhammapada

HAPPINESS is a Swedish sunset — it is there for all, but most of us look the other way and lose it.
Mark Twain

MERRILY, merrily whirled the wheels of the
    dizzying dances
Under the orchard-trees and down the path to the
    meadows;
Old folk and young together, and children
    mingled among them.
Henry Wadsworth Longfellow

THERE is something in the autumn that is
    native to my blood —
Touch of manner, hint of mood;
And my heart is like a rhyme,
With the yellow and the purple and the crimson
    keeping time.

The scarlet of the maples can shake me like a cry
Of bugles going by.
And my lonely spirit thrills
To see the frosty asters like a smoke upon the hills.

There is something in October sets the gypsy blood astir;
We must rise and follow her,
When from every bit of flame
She calls and calls each vagabond by name.

Bliss Carman

O! Joyous day! O! Smile of God
To hearten all who toil and plod;
We hail thee, Conqueror and King!
We hug our golden chains and sing:
   "Good morning!"

Thomas Augustin Daly

The haunts of happiness are varied, but I have more often found her among little children, home firesides, and country houses than anywhere else.
Sydney Smith

Happiness depends more upon the internal frame of a person's mind, than on the externals in the world.

Show not yourself glad at the misfortune of another, though he were your enemy.

Do not express joy before one sick or in pain, for that contrary passion will aggravate his misery.
George Washington
[from his Copy book]

To weep for joy is a kind of manna.
George Herbert

... It is by believing, hoping, loving, and doing that man finds joy and peace.

>   *John Lancaster Spalding*

My crown is in my heart, not on my head;
Not deck'd with diamonds and Indian stones,
Nor to be seen: my crown is call'd content;
A crown it is that seldom kings enjoy.

>   *William Shakespeare*

A WALK! The atmosphere incredibly pure — a warm, caressing gentleness in the sunshine — joy in one's whole being. . . . Forgotten impressions of childhood and youth came back to me — all those indescribable effects wrought by color, shadow, sunlight, green hedges, and songs of birds, upon the soul just opening to poetry. I became young again, wondering, and simple, as

candor and ignorance are simple. I abandoned myself to life and to nature, and they cradled me with an infinite gentleness. To open one's heart in purity to this ever pure nature, to allow this immortal life of things to penetrate into one's soul, is at the same time to listen to the voice of God. Sensation may be a prayer, and self-abandonment an act of devotion.

Henri Amiel

SOUND, sound the clarion, fill the fife!
 To all the sensual world proclaim,
One crowded hour of glorious life
 Is worth an age without a name.

Sir Walter Scott

SWEETS with sweets war not, joy delights in joy.
William Shakespeare

The sea! the sea! the open sea!
The blue, the fresh, the ever free!
Without a mark, without a bound,
It runneth the earth's wide regions round;
It plays with the clouds; it mocks the skies;
Or like a cradled creature lies.

I'm on the sea! I'm on the sea!
I am where I would ever be;
With the blue above, and the blue below,
And silence wheresoe'er I go;
If a storm should come and awake the deep,
What matter? I shall ride and sleep.

I love, O, how I love to ride
On the fierce, foaming, bursting tide,
When every mad wave drowns the moon
Or whistles aloft his tempest tune,
And tells how goeth the world below,
And why the sou'west blasts do blow....

Bryan Waller Procter

PEOPLE are always good company when they are doing what they really enjoy.

Samuel Butler

HASTE thee, Nymph, and bring with thee
Jest and youthful Jollity,
Quips and Cranks and wanton Wiles,
Nods and Becks and Wreathèd Smiles,
Such as hang on Hebe's cheek,
And love to live in dimple sleek;
Sport that wrinkled Care derides,
And Laughter holding both his sides.
Come, and trip it as you go
On the light fantastic toe. . . .

John Milton

Do you count your birthdays thankfully?

Horace

When the green woods laugh with the voice of joy,
And the dimpling stream runs laughing by;
When the air does laugh with our merry wit,
And the green hill laughs with the noise of it;

When the meadows laugh with lively green,
And the grasshopper laughs in the merry scene,
When Mary and Susan and Emily
With their sweet round mouths sing
  "Ha, Ha, He!"

When the painted birds laugh in the shade,
Where our table with cherries and nuts is spread,
Come live, and be merry, and join with me,
To sing sweet chorus of "Ha, Ha, He!"

William Blake

A merry companion is music on a journey.

Anonymous

GRIEF can take care of itself, but to get full value of a joy you must have somebody to divide it with.

Mark Twain

THE habit of being happy enables one to be freed, or largely freed, from the domination of outward conditions.

Robert Louis Stevenson

THE most delicate, the most sensible of all pleasures, consists in promoting the pleasure of others.

Jean de La Bruyère

ONE should take good care not to grow too wise for so great a pleasure of life as laughter.

Joseph Addison